"White" Girl Speaks!

Powerful Words of Inspiration for Leadership and Success in your Life!

Adair f. White-johnson, Ph.D.

ADAIR WHITE JOHNSON
The Empowerment House & Johnson Tribe Publishing

Published by Johnson Tribe Publishing, LLC
Atlanta, GA

Johnson Tribe Publishing
P.O. Box 1587 Powder Springs Georgia 30127

Johnson Tribe Publishing materials may be purchased for education, business, or
promotional use. The author is also available for speaking engagements. For
information, please contact us at (888) 400-7302, email us at info@
johnsontribepublishing.com or visit us at www. JohnsonTribePublishing.com

Manufactured in the United States of America

10 9 8 7 6 5 4 3 2 1

FIRST EDITION – June 2015
Creative Direction: Adair F. White-johnson, Ph.D.
Graphic Design: Stacey Bowers, August Pride, LLC
Book Design: DZine by Kellie

Library of Congress Catalog Card Number:

ISBN-13: 978-0-9896733-1-0

USA $5.97
Canada $7.50

DEDICATION

This one is for my family and friends who read my motivational messages and let me know that my words make a difference in their lives. It makes a difference in *my* life to know this.

Introduction

Sometimes when we are searching for our "purpose" in life, we get "stuck" and feel as though no one understands our situation, pain, and our dreams. We feel as though as much as we try we just never seem to get it right. And sometimes because we keep doing the same thing over and over again we still don't get it right. I think that you can learn from your mistakes and use those mistakes as starting points towards change. Never embracing failure but knowing when to accept defeat and understanding what makes you weaker but also focusing on what makes you stronger.

You never skimp on challenges because you have invested your total self. It is the only way you can "get over things to keep it moving" and the only way that you can bounce back after hitting rock bottom. This coupled with the strength, and the faith that comes from your belief and commitment to a higher power can only empower you.

For me, it constantly means leaning on my shield of faith and understanding that God's plan for me is the only plan that will ultimately prevail. I often turn to motivational messages and quotes to give me that immediate reminder that I am a leader, and I am destined for success.

You see, throughout my life there have been experiences that have hurt me to the core, questioned my belief system and the importance of things and people in my life. But you know what? The one constant that has not changed throughout all of this has been my Faith.

Yes, Faith has always been the shield that I lean on for hope, mercy, grace and humility. It is the spirit that moves me and allows me to know that despite and in spite of whatever may be happening in my life, "everything will be alright."

Through this journey, I know that I have been bent but not broken, damaged but not destroyed and tried but never convicted of failure. I am still that foot soldier emerging from the trenches and that warrior ready to do battle with devils in disguise. And now I am ready to share and teach others how to push through the pain and convicts of conscience to follow their dreams, become resilient on the road to becoming empowered to become effective leaders.

Much of what I have written in this book is grounded in my own growth, healing process and quest to become a more effective and successful leader in my personal and my professional lives. My thoughts and my words are delivered from the crevices of my soul, birthed from the core of my existence, developed by my belief in the power of prayer and emerged from the strength of believing in who I am and what I do. The inspirational quotes in this book are designed to empower you to think about your life differently and to help you make choices that will lead you towards emotional prosperity because you deserve to be happy. Remember, "although you may not be where you want to be, you don't have to be where you used to be either."

"White" Girl Speaks!

Sometimes people *love* you
the best way they know how.

**But it's up to you to decide if you
will accept their type of love.**

Lesson:
Know how you want to be loved.

ECONOMIC
poverty does not dictate
INTELLECTUAL
impoverishment

LESSON:
Just because you may be "POOR"
doesn't mean you are "STUPID"

Never let your
disabilities "disable"
your abilities
or "limit" your
possibilities.

Lesson:
*Just because you may have a
disability doesn't mean that your life
doesn't have infinite possibilities.*

Just because you "THINK" it doesn't mean you have to "SAY" it.

and just because you say it doesn't make it the "truth!"

Lesson: Be careful what you say and who you say it to.

" I may not be
exactly where I
want to be, but I'm
not where I used
to be either. "

LESSON: CHANGE BEGINS WITH YOUR PERSPECTIVE FIRST.

BE STILL.
Listen.
BE OBEDIENT.

God is always speaking to you. His volume never changes. His time is consistent, and his voice is electrifying. It's just the noise around you that deafens your ears to what he is saying.

Lesson: Silence the voices that interfere with God's message to you.

YES!

Faith moves
mountains, but
it takes prayer
to believe that it
can and will.

Lesson:
Prayer changes everything.

PAN I AM NOT MY

If you keep thinking it, eventually you will

BELIEVE it.

If you keep saying it, eventually someone else will

HEAR it.

But if you keep doing it, then it becomes reality and everyone will

SEE it.

**Lesson: Think It . Say. It Do It.
That's the only way dreams come true.**

> **If you are in the same position this year that you promised yourself you wouldn't be in last year, then whatever you were doing *DID NOT* work!!!!**

Lesson: Accept what you have done and what you failed to do and then create a plan to make a positive difference in your own life...

"WHAT HAPPENS TO A DREAM DEFERRED? NOTHING. ABSOLUTELY NOTHING.

WORK YOUR DREAM SO YOU CAN LIVE YOUR DREAM"

Lesson: Dreams don't come with a warranty or guarantee so you have to "make" it happen not just "let" it happen.

Some situations in life are

MIND
OVER
MATTER

If you don't **"MIND"**, then it really should not **"MATTER."**

Lesson: Pick and choose your battles.

I am already
"So Much,"
but I also know that
I am destined to be
"So Much More..."

Lesson:
Self-confidence, self-love, and
self-motivation are the first steps
in following your dreams.

Find your center and build everything positive around it.

Lesson: You may not be the "center" of the universe, but you should be the "center" of your own world.

Some of us choose to live in a **"Comfortable Hell"** because we think it is easier than living the truth in our **"Uncomfortable Heaven."**
(adapted from T. Jones)

The sad part of it is that many of us don't know the difference.

Lesson: Know your address...Know where you choose to live.

it ain't over TIL GOD says IT is

You'll never know what your *emotional & psychological* sobriety is dependent upon if you are always intoxicated with old hurt.

Lesson:

Detox your mind, body and soul from pain. **Let it go! *Get Over It!***

SOME SAY THAT
"IGNORANCE IS BLISS"
BUT I SAY THAT IGNORANCE IS JUST
"STUPIDITY IN THE RAW"
LESSON: IGNORANT PEOPLE ALWAYS SAY STUPID THINGS. EXPECT IT.

Closing your eyes and pretending that your problems don't exist is like facing the mirror backwards and pretending to be someone else.

Lesson: Face your life. Face your problems. Face who you really are. It's the only way to make true changes in your life.

IF YOU ALLOW
FEAR
to paralyze your

faith

then you may never
WALK
again...

WHEN YOU FINALLY
ACCEPT THAT
GOD IS THE ONLY
TRUTH, THEN YOU'LL
ALREADY KNOW THAT
THE DEVIL IS A LIAR.

LESSON: YOU CAN'T HAVE IT BOTH WAYS.

A LIE WILL NEVER
BE THE **TRUTH** NO
MATTER WHICH WAY
YOU TELL IT.

I think I can......

I think I can......

I think I can......

Because I have to.

Lesson: The *Power* of *Positive* Thinking.
excerpt from "The Little Engine that Could"

SOMETIMES I JUST WISH THAT CERTAIN FEELINGS WOULD JUST DISAPPEAR.

POOF!
BE GONE!

?

IF YOU ASK ME THE QUESTION THEN BE PREPARED FOR THE ANSWER.

*Lesson: Know that **"The Truth Will Set You Free"** But it also can hurt. Be ready.*

STOP THINKING ABOUT ANY SKELETONS IN MY CLOSET WHEN YOUR ENTIRE LIFE IS ROOTED IN THE CEMETERY

Just because someone is sitting on your front "row"
doesn't mean they are clapping for you.
Scan your audience for those who have
been giving you a standing ovation all along.

Lesson: Look beyond the orchestra seats for your support group.

You are only
TREATED
the way you
ALLOW
yourself to be treated.

LESSON: Figure out how you want others to treat you but remember it works both ways... Treat others as you would want to be treated.

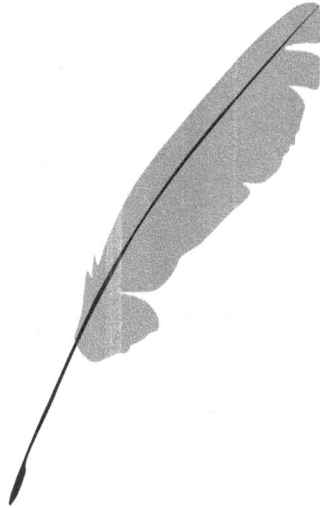

To deny who you are today
is to deny who you are
destined to become tomorrow.

Lesson: *"To thine own self be true"*
"Shakespearean Quote"

YOU OWN THE POWER OF CHANGE

SO STOP COMPLAINING

AND CHANGE IT !

Lesson: Make a difference in your life by making a change in your life.

THERE IS
ABSOLUTELY
NOTHING **RIGHT**
ABOUT BEING
WRONG. AND JUST
BECAUSE YOU
THINK YOU ARE
RIGHT, DOESN'T
MAKE EVERYONE
ELSE WRONG.

LESSON: 2 WRONGS DON'T MAKE A RIGHT.

IF FAITH CAN MOVE MOUNTAINS THEN IT HAS NO PROBLEM PULLING YOU OUT OF A VALLEY

MY

faith

IS STRONGER THAN MY

pain

WHEN YOU FEEL HELPLESS AND HOPELESS REMEMBER THE POWER OF PRAYER.

LESSON: PRAYER DOES MAKE A DIFFERENCE.

I am worth releasing all people and all things that are not worthy of me.

LET

THEM

GO!!!!

You never realize how **special** today is until you don't have that loved one to share it with anymore.

Lesson: Love who you love today because tomorrow is too far away. Anything can happen before then.

IT'S
NOT
JUST
WHAT
YOU
SAY
BUT
RATHER
WHAT
YOU
DO THAT MAKES THE DIFFERENCE
IN YOUR HAPPINESS.

LESSON
JUST DO IT.

I *love* me the best way I know how but when I know better, I do better...

Lesson: Self-love is a true love...
Don't depend on others to give it to you... They can't.

You have to "Work your dream to Live your dream."

Lesson: Dreams do not come with a warranty or guarantee.

Just because you "walk away" doesn't mean you have "given up."

It simply means you made a choice.

Lesson: Sometimes you just gotta take a walk.

I may be **sorry** for what I *did* but
I'm **NEVER SORRY** for *who* I am.

*Lesson: God created me therefore I'm already
who I am supposed to be.*

"THINKING YOU CAN'T DO IT IS WHAT MAKES YOU LOSE. WHILE KNOWING YOU WILL DO IT MAKES YOU WIN!"

LESSON: GET YOUR MIND RIGHT!

You think you've seen the **BEST** of me?

NAHHHHHH...................

The Best is yet to come 'cuz **GOD** aint
done
with
me
yet!!!

**Lesson: Self-Confidence and Faith
are the cornerstones to Success.**

Following a rainbow without a pot of gold at the end is like driving down a "dead-end" street... Once you reach the end there's no place left to go.

Lesson: Following your **heart, soul, mind and faith** will always take you to an open road.

DIVORCE

YOU NEED A DIVORCE!!!!

Divorce from anything that causes.

Heartache
PAIN

Negativity
TOXIC PEOPLE

Toxic Situations

Lesson: File for Divorce papers today!

DIVORCE

GOD told me he wasn't finished with me yet...
In fact he said "I've only just begun."

And with that, he gave me new dreams to fulfill...

Lesson: Dreams are not just for sleeping.
They are for living too.

66 SO EVEN IF YOU THINK
THAT YOU ARE JUST

ORDINARY

YOU SHOULD ALWAYS BE

EXTRAORDINARY

ABOUT IT. 99

Lesson: We are all born with "gifts" but
it is up to us to use them as "talents."

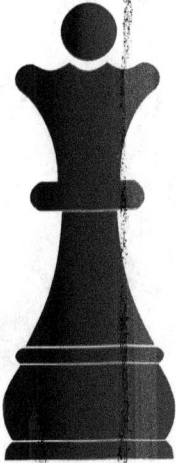

Sometimes you just have to be **STILL** in order to know what your next move will be.

Lesson: You don't always have to "move" to go places.

KNOWING
WHO YOU ARE
IS THE FIRST STEP IN
FIGURING
OUT WHAT YOU WANT

❤ ✿ ❤ ✿ ❤

LESSON: ONE STEP AT A TIME

WHEN WE ARE CHILDREN WE DREAM ABOUT **"THE FUTURE."**

WHEN WE ARE TEENAGERS WE BEGIN TO WORK TOWARDS **"THE FUTURE."**

BUT WHEN WE ARE ADULTS WE SHOULD BECOME **"THE FUTURE."**

THOSE WHO ARE STILL DREAMING AND NOT WORKING TOWARDS THE FUTURE ARE STILL LIVING IN THE PAST...

LESSON: LIVE IN YOUR PURPOSE SO YOU WON'T DIE WHILE YOU ARE EXISTING IN THE PAST.

JUST WHEN YOU THINK
YOU NEED GOD THE
LEAST IS WHEN YOU
REALLY NEED HIM
THE MOST.

LESSON: YOU ARE NOTHING
WITHOUT GOD... DON'T FORGET IT.

No one ever gave me anything but a

Chance

I took that chance and made it an

Opportunity

And I used that to make
my dreams come true.

I ALREADY KNOW THAT I AM

"SO MUCH"

BUT AM LOOKING FORWARD TO BEING

"SO MUCH MORE!"

LESSON: THE POWER OF PURPOSE, PLANNING,
PERSISTENCE AND POSITIVE THINKING...

So today is a ROUGH day for you.

I UNDERSTAND.

But tomorrow is
only a day away.

What's the plan?

Nah,
YOU can't steal the joy from
MY heart because you
didn't put it there in
the first place!!!!

Lesson: Go and be miserable by your damn self.

Dr. Adair Speaks

There will always be some folks who will *never* like your posts, favorite your tweets, **"follow"** you, or request to be your friend... no matter what you post and share.

SO WHAT?

Lesson: Don't look for approval through social media --- look in the mirror first to find affirmation in your life.

GET OVER IT!

I AM. I CAN. I WILL. I DO.

JUST BECAUSE I BELIEVE.

Sometimes
YOU
Can't Take The
PAIN
Away Because You
DIDN'T
Put It There

Thanks for trying though...

If we allow ourselves to

DREAM} it
n. [dreem]

then why won't we allow ourselves to

DO} it
v. [doo]

I'M NOT AFRAID OF MY DREAMS.
I'M AFRAID TO STOP HAVING DREAMS.

I'VE BEEN

'lucky'

AND I'VE BEEN

'BLESSED'

BUT

I'LL TAKE

'BLESSED'

OVER

'lucky'

ANYTIME

When it's just too hard to

"PUSH THROUGH THE PAIN"

ALONE....

| Remember... | PATIENCE, POSITIVITY, & PRAYER |

gives you the power you need

{ to persevere... }

> Sometimes all we get is a "CHANCE," but it is up to us to make it an "OPPORTUNITY."
>
> Sometimes all we get is the "DREAM," but it's up to us to make it a "REALITY."
>
> And sometimes all we get is "AIR," and we just have to allow ourselves to "BREATHE."

Sometimes you just need to be **STILL** to hear **God's** words.

IF WE DON'T
WANT FOLKS
KNOWING OUR **BIZNESS**

THEN JUST STOP TELLIN' IT!!!!

OR, **POSTING** IT!!!!

Lesson: Not everything belongs
on Social Media.

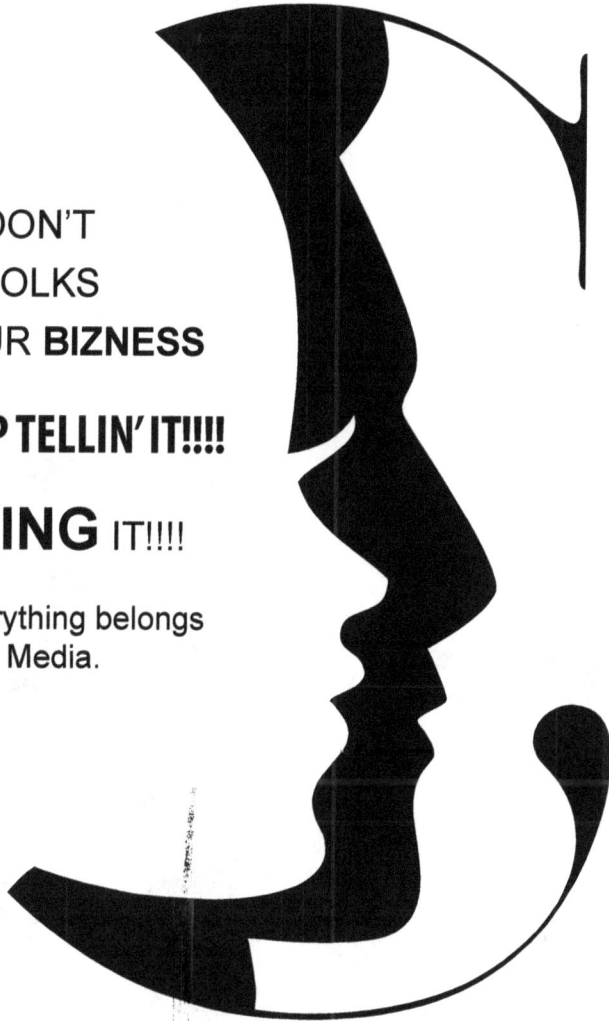

NOTE:

Just becasue YOU decided NOT to follow your dreams doesn't mean you get to belittle, degrade, discourage or block mine!

Lesson: If you don't support me then stay away from me. I am more than what you think because I Am my dreams and I LIVE my reality.

"White" Girl Speaks!

Just when I think everything is going WRONG in my life, I look up and I'm reminded that everything is going to be ALRIGHT.

NOTHING + NOTHING = NOTHING

YOU GOTTA DO SOMETHING TO GET A DIFFERENT ANSWER.

LESSON: GET YOUR BUTT UP SO YOU CAN "WORK A DREAM TO LIVE A DREAM!"

> **I DON'T WORRY ABOUT WHAT OTHERS SAY ABOUT ME** because I already know what **GOD** says **TO** me...
>
> Lesson: God always has the last word.

Faith
has no filter.
No shade
It's ## Raw.
It's ## Real.

It is what it is. No explanations needed.

NOTE TO SELF:

Do one more thing today than I normally do to make my dreams come true.

I have to "Work a Dream to Live a Dream."

NO

THE WORD "NO" IS A COMPLETE SENTENCE... YOU DON'T NEED "BECAUSE" OR "AND" TO VALIDATE IT...

You don't need a MAGIC WAND to bring Magic into your life... They're called *Blessings* and all you have to do is Believe and ask God for his favor...

#notricks

SOMETIMES THE PEOPLE WHO **SAY** THEY LOVE YOU THE MOST WILL **SHOW** YOU THE LEAST.

Praying for Perspective about
your Passion also Prepares you
for the Pursuit of your Purpose.

I AM NOT MY PAIN

If you allow **FEAR}**
n. [feer]
to paralyze your
FAITH}
n. [feyth]
then you may never walk again...

If you are only dreaming while you are sleeping then you must be exhausted trying to figure out your purpose while you are awake.

Lesson: Dreams are not just for sleeping... They are the starting points towards change in your life. Make sure you are still "DAYDREAMING."

Knowing
WHO
you are is the
first step in
figuring out
WHAT
you want...

Lesson: One step at a time...

"

SOMETIMES I'M SCARED OF MY DREAMS...
BUT THEN I REALIZE THAT THE

fear of faliure

IS THE REAL NIGHTMARE.

#keepdreamin'

"

IT
AIN'T
OVER
TILL
GOD
SAYS
IT IS...

TOXIC PEOPLE ARE LIKE WEEDS GROWING IN GRASS...
THEY WILL BECOME TALLER AND STRONGER IF YOU DON'T PULL THEM OUT..

LESSON: BEGIN PULLING THE WEEDS OUT OF YOUR GARDEN NOW...

SOME RELATIONSHIPS ARE SO EXHAUSTING..

AND SO TIRING THAT THEY WEAR YOU OUT EACH TIME YOU DEAL WITH THE PERSON...

LESSON:
HMMM...
I WOULD
RATHER TAKE
A GOOD NAP
THEN DEAL
WITH THESE
FOLKS AT
LEAST I
WILL BE
WELL-RESTED
AFTERWARDS

What I learned today:

"Faith is not absent of Fear..."

But you still push through the pain, walk through the path of doubt and confusion anyway because you know that through it all, Faith is on your side...

If you say I
"COULDA WOULDA SHOULDA,"
too much then you probably never did, and never will.

Lesson: Sometimes action does speak louder than words.

> **"** IT'S ALREADY BAD ENOUGH
> WHEN WE THINK THAT
> WE'VE DONE "EVERYTHING"
> FOR SOMEONE AND FEELING
> LIKE WE HAVE RECEIVED
> "NOTHING IN RETURN..."
>
> BUT IT IS WORSE IF IT'S
> ACTUALLY TRUE... **"**
>
> LESSON: YOU ARE ONLY TREATED AS YOU
> ALLOW YOURSELF TO BE TREATED.

YOU MAY *wound* **MY FEELINGS WITH THE** *truth* but you will definitely kill MY TRUST, HOPE, FAITH AND LOVE *with* lies.

LESSON: THE TRUTH MAY HURT BUT IT WORKS.

If you keep living a
"COULDA WOULDA SHOULDA„
existence then your future will become a
"I COULDN'T WOULDN'T and DIDN'T„
type of life...

Lesson: Doing nothing brings you nothing.

Feelings by themselves
are never right or
wrong...
it's what you DO with
them that makes them
right or wrong...

Lesson: Just because you FEEL it, doesn't
mean you have to DO it.

Sometimes the scariest thing about change is the *"thought"* of changing and not the change itself.

Lesson: You first have to change the way you think before you change the way you behave.

"Sometimes we search all over the house looking for that "last" dollar we think we lost...

Only to find 4 quarters laying right on the table..."

Lesson: Sometimes what we need is right before us but we just don't recognize it.

I've learned that just because

you want to

"DO" | right

doesn't | **mean you always want to**

{ **"be"** } right

But! | if {"being"} leads to {"doing"}

then they just have to

GET OVER IT!

Lesson: Never apologize for doing the right thing for the reasons at the right times. Always try to "Do the right thing."

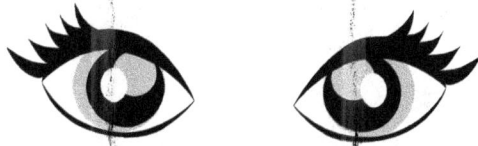

The best part of the morning is opening my eyes.

The next best part is realizing I am still alive.
But the BIGGEST best part is knowing that
my GOD made it all possible.

Lesson: Remember you are blessed just to see another day.

"Never let your *Disabilities* disable your
Abilities or limit your *Possibilities*...
Never let your *Downfalls* determine
your *Destiny* because your *Dreams*
decide your *Destination*."

Lesson: The sky is the limit for your dreams because the "clouds belong to you.... When you are not moving, you are flying."

About The Author

Dr. Adair is an Empowerologist, Life Strengthener, Publisher and Professor in Atlanta, Georgia. She is also the author of numerous articles, curricula, and books, including "Get Over It! How to Bounce Back after Hitting Rock Bottom" and the bestsellers "How to Get Over It in 30 Days" Parts I and II. Her book, "Get Over It! 7 Steps to Living Well with Lupus" was a #1 Amazon bestseller list and has remained on the list for five months.

In addition, she has created an award-winning leadership and personal development curriculum and program for teens that is aligned with the national Common Core Standards and the American School Counselor Association National Model Standards. She earned her Ph.D. from the University at Buffalo and holds a master's degree in the counseling field. Dr. Adair is married and the mother of five children.

Other Titles by Dr. Adair:
"How to Get Over It in 30 Days" Part I
"How to Get Over It in 30 Days" Part II
"Get Over It!" How to Bounce Back After Hitting Rock Bottom
"Get Over It" How to Bounce Back After Hitting Rock Bottom for Teens
"Get Over It! 7 Steps to Living Well with Lupus"
"Go Hard and Stumble Softly"

www.ingramcontent.com/pod-product-compliance
Lightning Source LLC
Chambersburg PA
CBHW080523030426

42337CB00023B/4616